18092

Albuquerque Academy

The Pinnacled Tower

SELECTED POEMS BY

THOMAS HARDY

EDITED BY HELEN PLOTZ

WOOD ENGRAVINGS BY

CLARE LEIGHTON

MACMILLAN PUBLISHING CO., INC.
NEW YORK

Macmillan Publishing Co., Inc.
866 Third Avenue, New York, N.Y. 10022
Printed in the United States of America

10 9 8 7 6 5 4 3 2 1

Reprinted with permission of Macmillan Publishing Co., Inc.,
from *Collected Poems* by Thomas Hardy:
Copyright 1925 by Macmillan Publishing Co., Inc.,
Copyright renewed 1953 by Lloyds Bank Limited—"Farmer
Dunman's Funeral," "Horses Aboard," "The Pat of Butter,"
"She Opened the Door," and "Waiting Both."
Copyright 1928 by Florence E. Hardy and Sydney E.
Cockerell, Copyright renewed 1956 by Lloyds Bank Limited—
"Christmas: 1924," "I Watched a Blackbird," "A Necessi-
tarian's Epitaph," "Thoughts at Midnight," "To Louisa in the
Lane," and "Yuletide in a Younger World."

Library of Congress Cataloging in Publication Data
Hardy, Thomas, 1840–1928. The pinnacled tower.
[1. English poetry] I. Leighton, Clare Veronica Hope, date,
illus. II. Title.
PR4742.P58   821'.8   74–14836   ISBN 0-02-742630-0

EDITOR'S NOTE

When notes follow the poems, those set in italic type
are Hardy's own; those in roman type are mine.

In remembrance of a journey in Wessex
and of Milton who shared with me his love
for the inward and outward landscape
of Thomas Hardy

CONTENTS

INTRODUCTION

Thomas Hardy was a poet who wrote novels. So he thought of himself, although the world thought otherwise and honored him most for his novels of Wessex life and the unforgettable characters he created.

He was born on June 2, 1840, three years after Queen Victoria's coronation, and died on January 11, 1928. He was the first-born child of Thomas and Jemina Hardy of Stinsford, Dorset, in the south of England. During his long life, although he lived for several years in London, he was always a man of Dorset, which was once part of the Anglo-Saxon Kingdom of Wessex, the domain of King Lear. Indeed it is not hard to picture this foolish fond old man as a character in one of Hardy's novels or as the subject of one of his sad and ironic poems.

Hardy had a strong sense of family and of place. He was painfully aware of the passing of the old order, of a life rooted in the seasons and in the soil. From his parents, he inherited a love of music, of nature and of reading. His mother, in long walks over the moors, imbued the boy with a love of the austere and majestic landscape of Dorset. Young Thomas liked to fiddle and to dance, encouraged by the elder Thomas, who, like his own father before him, was a church musician. By profession, Thomas the elder was a master builder, so it seemed natural enough for Thomas, after his school years, to be apprenticed to an architect. He had had vague dreams of entering the church and was a profound student of the Bible. Although his knowledge of the Bible shines through all of his poems, they reveal such deep agnosticism that it is doubtful that he would ever have taken or kept to Holy Orders.

The young architect went to London to complete his training. There he began to dream not of building and restoring churches and houses but of writing. A few poems and his first published novel, *Desperate Remedies* (1871), were written between the intervals of work in London and church restoration in Dorset and in Cornwall in the West of England.

On March 7, 1870, Thomas was sent to St. Juliot Rectory in Cornwall. This journey, the most fateful in his life, is described in one of his loveliest poems, "When I Set Out for Lyonnesse." Emma Lavinia Gifford, sister-in-law of the rector, opened the door to him—the door to the house, the door to the West and the door to all of their lives thereafter. It was a long courtship. They walked together in Cornwall and explored the old churches. Long letters passed between them and Thomas sent his manuscripts to Emma, who made fair copies for him. Shortly after their meeting, Hardy abandoned architecture and began his career as a novelist. In September of 1874, they were married in London and soon afterward returned to Dorset where, after another stay in London, they later built a house called Max Gate.

The marriage, so auspiciously begun, was dissolved by Emma's death in 1912, but long before that there was estrangement between them. Hardy's greatest joys and deepest griefs arose from his marriage. Fundamental incompatability between the two did not become apparent in their early years together and was more or less successfully concealed from most of their friends and acquaintances. There was never a time when Emma was not Hardy's "dearest Emmy" nor a time when Emma did not feel a deep and abiding love for her husband, but "autumn wrought division." It is not for us to judge between them; perhaps it is fairest to say that each was, in biblical phrase, not "an help meet" for the other.

Immediately after Emma's death, Hardy poured out in

matchless poetry all of their story. He told of their courtship and marriage, their divisions and misunderstandings, and then, unsparing of himself, described his remorse and his unquenched love. I have chosen some among these poems. I hope that my readers will find and read them all.

There was one circumstance of their lives which brought joy to Emma shortly before her death. Hardy was awarded the Order of Merit. This Order, founded by King Edward VII, is limited to twenty-four members chosen for "unusually deserving achievement in the promotion of the arts, literature and science."

Some time before Emma's death, the Hardys had become acquainted with a young woman named Florence Emily Dugdale. In 1914, she was married to Thomas Hardy. The marriage was serene and rewarding, and if it lacked the fire of youth, it lacked its heartbreak as well. As Hardy himself said, "Two bright-souled women clave to him." He died at eighty-eight, full of years and honor, and his ashes were buried in Westminster Abbey with all the glorious pomp of a state funeral. His heart is interred in Stinsford churchyard.

I share Hardy's belief that he was first of all a poet. During his lifetime, his novels made him famous. The last two, *Tess of the D'Urbervilles* and *Jude the Obscure,* were vehemently attacked and as vehemently defended in the pulpit and the press, sometimes for the wrong reasons. After *Jude the Obscure,* Hardy devoted himself to poetry and to the completion of *The Dynasts,* an epic drama of the Napoleonic Wars, published in three parts in 1904, 1906 and 1908. The themes of his novels are the themes of his poems—the conflict between the old and the new, the indifference of the gods, the dislocations of war, the village tragedies, the satires of circumstance. These pervade the poems as they do the novels. He has had a great influence on the poets of our day, first among them W. H. Auden. Hardy's own voice is unmistakable; a sometimes surprising juxtaposition of colloquialism and majestic biblical phrases and the use of both archaic and invented words combine to make him unique among English poets.

The poet reveals himself to us again and again as sensitive, sometimes rebellious, sometimes resigned, and above all compassionate, not only to his fellow-beings but to the humblest of God's creatures.

Hardy's character as a man and as a poet is, I believe, best summed up by the poem he wrote in anticipation of death:

AFTERWARDS

When the Present has latched its postern behind my tremulous
    stay,
  And the May month flaps its glad green leaves like wings,
Delicate-filmed as new-spun silk, will the neighbours say,
  "He was a man who used to notice such things"?

If it be in the dusk when, like an eyelid's soundless blink,
  The dewfall-hawk comes crossing the shades to alight
Upon the wind-warped upland thorn, a gazer may think,
  "To him this must have been a familiar sight."

If I pass during some nocturnal blackness, mothy and warm,
  When the hedgehog travels furtively over the lawn,
One may say, "He strove that such innocent creatures should
    come to no harm,
  But he could do little for them; and now he is gone."

If, when hearing that I have been stilled at last, they stand at
    the door,
  Watching the full-starred heavens that winter sees,
Will this thought rise on those who will meet my face no
    more,
  "He was one who had an eye for such mysteries"?

And will any say when my bell of quittance is heard in the
    gloom,
  And a crossing breeze cuts a pause in its outrollings,
Till they rise again, as they were a new bell's boom,
  "He hears it not now, but used to notice such things"?

New York   HELEN PLOTZ
1975

The Year's Awakening
THE WORLD OF NATURE

THE YEAR'S AWAKENING

How do you know that the pilgrim track
Along the belting zodiac
Swept by the sun in his seeming rounds
Is traced by now to the Fishes' bounds
And into the Ram, when weeks of cloud
Have wrapt the sky in a clammy shroud,
And never as yet a tinct of spring
Has shown in the Earth's apparelling;
    O vespering bird, how do you know,
      How do you know?

How do you know, deep underground,
Hid in your bed from sight and sound,
Without a turn in temperature,
With weather life can scarce endure,
That light has won a fraction's strength,
And day put on some moments' length,
Whereof in merest rote will come,
Weeks hence, mild airs that do not numb,
    O crocus root, how do you know,
      How do you know?

February 1910.

3

WEATHERS

I

This is the weather the cuckoo likes,
  And so do I;
When showers betumble the chestnut spikes,
  And nestlings fly:
And the little brown nightingale bills his best,
And they sit outside at "The Travellers' Rest,"
And maids come forth sprig-muslin drest,
And citizens dream of the south and west,
  And so do I.

II

This is the weather the shepherd shuns,
  And so do I;
When beeches drip in browns and duns,
  And thresh, and ply;
And hill-hid tides throb, throe on throe,
And meadow rivulets overflow,
And drops on gate-bars hang in a row,
And rooks in families homeward go,
  And so do I.

"IF IT'S EVER SPRING AGAIN"
(Song)

If it's ever spring again,
      Spring again,
I shall go where went I when
Down the moor-cock splashed, and hen,
Seeing me not, amid their flounder,
Standing with my arm around her;
If it's ever spring again,
      Spring again,
I shall go where went I then.

If it's ever summer-time,
      Summer-time,
With the hay crop at the prime,
And the cuckoos—two—in rhyme,
As they used to be, or seemed to,
We shall do as long we've dreamed to,
If it's ever summer-time,
      Summer-time,
With the hay, and bees achime.

"THE WIND BLEW WORDS"

The wind blew words along the skies,
   And these it blew to me
Through the wide dusk: "Lift up your eyes,
   Behold this troubled tree,
Complaining as it sways and plies;
   It is a limb of thee.

"Yea, too, the creatures sheltering round—
   Dumb figures, wild and tame,
Yea, too, thy fellows who abound—
   Either of speech the same
Or far and strange—black, dwarfed, and browned,
   They are stuff of thy own frame."

I moved on in a surging awe
   Of inarticulateness
At the pathetic Me I saw
   In all his huge distress,
Making self-slaughter of the law
   To kill, break, or suppress.

THE IVY-WIFE

I longed to love a full-boughed beech
    And be as high as he:
I stretched an arm within his reach,
    And signalled unity.
But with his drip he forced a breach,
    And tried to poison me.

I gave the grasp of partnership
    To one of other race—
A plane: he barked him strip by strip
    From upper bough to base;
And me therewith; for gone my grip,
    My arms could not enlace.

In new affection next I strove
    To coll an ash I saw,
And he in trust received my love;
    Till with my soft green claw
I cramped and bound him as I wove . . .
    Such was my love: ha-ha!

By this I gained his strength and height
    Without his rivalry.
But in my triumph I lost sight
    Of afterhaps. Soon he,
Being bark-bound, flagged, snapped, fell outright,
    And in his fall felled me!

AN AUGUST MIDNIGHT

I
A shaded lamp and a waving blind,
And the beat of a clock from a distant floor:
On this scene enter—winged, horned, and spined—
A longlegs, a moth, and a dumbledore;*
While 'mid my page there idly stands
A sleepy fly, that rubs its hands . . .

II
Thus meet we five, in this still place,
At this point of time, at this point in space.
—My guests besmear my new-penned line,
Or bang at the lamp and fall supine.
"God's humblest, they!" I muse. Yet why?
They know Earth-secrets that know not I.

Max Gate, 1899.

---

* A bumblebee.

CHORUS OF THE YEARS*

Yes, the coneys are scared by the thud of hoofs,
And their white scuts flash at their vanishing heels,
And swallows abandon the hamlet roofs.

The mole's tunnelled chambers are crushed by wheels,
The lark's eggs scattered, their owners fled;
And the hedgehog's household the sapper unseals.

The snail draws in at the terrible tread,
But in vain; he is crushed by the felloe-rim;
The worm asks what can be overhead,

And wriggles deep from a scene so grim,
And guesses him safe; for he does not know
What a foul red flood will be soaking him!

Beaten about by the heel and toe
Are butterflies, sick of the day's long rheum,
To die of a worse than the weather-foe.

Trodden and bruised to a miry tomb
Are ears that have greened but will never be gold,
And flowers in the bud that will never bloom.

---

* Immediately before Waterloo. From *The Dynasts*.

HORSES ABOARD

Horses in horseclothes stand in a row
On board the huge ship, that at last lets go:
Whither are they sailing? They do not know,
Nor what for, nor how.—
                They are horses of war,
And are going to where there is fighting afar;
But they gaze through their eye-holes unwitting they are,
And that in some wilderness, gaunt and ghast,
Their bones will bleach ere a year has passed,
And the item be as "war-waste" classed.—
And when the band booms, and the folk say "Good-bye!"
And the shore slides astern, they appear wrenched awry
From the scheme Nature planned for them,—wondering why.

THE FALLOW DEER AT
THE LONELY HOUSE

One without looks in to-night
    Through the curtain-chink
From the sheet of glistening white;
One without looks in to-night
    As we sit and think
    By the fender-brink.

We do not discern those eyes
    Watching in the snow;
Lit by lamps of rosy dyes
We do not discern those eyes
    Wondering, aglow,
    Fourfooted, tiptoe.

THE SELFSAME SONG

A bird sings the selfsame song,
With never a fault in its flow,
That we listened to here those long
    Long years ago.

A pleasing marvel is how
A strain of such rapturous rote
Should have gone on thus till now
    Unchanged in a note!

—But it's not the selfsame bird.—
No: perished to dust is he. . . .
As also are those who heard
    That song with me.

"I WATCHED A BLACKBIRD"

I watched a blackbird on a budding sycamore
One Easter Day, when sap was stirring twigs to the core;
    I saw his tongue, and crocus-coloured bill
    Parting and closing as he turned his trill;
    Then he flew down, seized on a stem of hay,
And upped to where his building scheme was under way,
As if so sure a nest were never shaped on spray.

THE SPRING CALL

Down Wessex way, when spring's a-shine,
    The blackbird's "pret-ty de-urr!"
In Wessex accents marked as mine
    Is heard afar and near.

He flutes it strong, as if in song
    No R's of feebler tone
Than his appear in "pretty dear,"
    Have blackbirds ever known.

Yet they pipe "prattie deerh!" I glean,
    Beneath a Scottish sky,
And "pehty de-aw!" amid the treen
    Of Middlesex or nigh.

While some folk say—perhaps in play—
    Who know the Irish isle,
'Tis "purrity dare!" in treeland there
    When songsters would beguile.

Well: I'll say what the listening birds
    Say, hearing "pret-ty de-urr!"—
However strangers sound such words,
    That's how we sound them here.

Yes, in this clime at pairing time,
    As soon as eyes can see her
At dawn of day, the proper way
    To call is "pret-ty de-urr!"

BIRDS AT WINTER NIGHTFALL
(Triolet)

Around the house the flakes fly faster,
And all the berries now are gone
From holly and cotonea-aster
Around the house. The flakes fly!—faster
Shutting indoors that crumb-outcaster
We used to see upon the lawn
Around the house. The flakes fly faster,
And all the berries now are gone!

Max Gate.

THE REMINDER

While I watch the Christmas blaze
Paint the room with ruddy rays,
Something makes my vision glide
To the frosty scene outside.

There, to reach a rotting berry,
Toils a thrush,—constrained to very
Dregs of food by sharp distress,
Taking such with thankfulness.

Why, O starving bird, when I
One day's joy would justify,
And put misery out of view,
Do you make me notice you!

THE PUZZLED GAME-BIRDS
(Triolet)

They are not those who used to feed us
When we were young—they cannot be—
These shapes that now bereave and bleed us?
They are not those who used to feed us,
For did we then cry, they would heed us.
—If hearts can house such treachery
They are not those who used to feed us
When we were young—they cannot be!

THE DARKLING THRUSH

I leant upon a coppice gate
    When Frost was spectre-gray,
And Winter's dregs made desolate
    The weakening eye of day.
The tangled bine-stems scored the sky
    Like strings of broken lyres,
And all mankind that haunted nigh
    Had sought their household fires.

The land's sharp features seemed to be
    The Century's corpse outleant,
His crypt the cloudy canopy,
    The wind his death-lament.
The ancient pulse of germ and birth
    Was shrunken hard and dry,
And every spirit upon earth
    Seemed fervourless as I.

At once a voice arose among
    The bleak twigs overhead
In a full-hearted evensong
    Of joy illimited;
An aged thrush, frail, gaunt, and small,
    In blast-beruffled plume,
Had chosen thus to fling his soul
    Upon the growing gloom.

So little cause for carolings
    Of such ecstatic sound
Was written on terrestrial things
    Afar or nigh around,
That I could think there trembled through
    His happy good-night air
Some blessed Hope, whereof he knew
    And I was unaware.

December 1900.

THE BLINDED BIRD

So zestfully canst thou sing?
And all this indignity,
With God's consent, on thee!
Blinded ere yet a-wing
By the red-hot needle thou,
I stand and wonder how
So zestfully thou canst sing!

Resenting not such wrong,
Thy grievous pain forgot,
Eternal dark thy lot,
Groping thy whole life long,
After that stab of fire;
Enjailed in pitiless wire;
Resenting not such wrong!

Who hath charity? This bird.
Who suffereth long and is kind,
Is not provoked, though blind
And alive ensepulchred?
Who hopeth, endureth all things?
Who thinketh no evil, but sings?
Who is divine? This bird.

Past Things Retold

FRIENDS AND FAMILY

ONE WE KNEW

(M. H. 1772–1857)*

She told how they used to form for the country dances—
    "The Triumph," "The New-rigged Ship"—
To the light of the guttering wax in the panelled manses
    And in cots to the blink of a dip.

She spoke of the wild "poussetting" and "allemanding"
    On carpet, on oak, and on sod;
And the two long rows of ladies and gentlemen standing,
    And the figures the couples trod.

She showed us the spot where the maypole was yearly planted,
    And where the bandsmen stood
While breeched and kerchiefed partners whirled, and panted
    To choose each other for good.

She told of that far-back day when they learnt astounded
    Of the death of the King of France:
Of the Terror; and then of Bonaparte's unbounded
    Ambition and arrogance.

Of how his threats woke warlike preparations
    Along the southern strand,
And how each night brought tremors and trepidations
    Lest morning should see him land.

She said she had often heard the gibbet creaking
    As it swayed in the lightning flash,
Had caught from the neighbouring town a small child's
    shrieking
    At the cart-tail under the lash. . . .

---

* Hardy's grandmother.

With cap-framed face and long gaze into the embers—
　　We seated around her knees—
She would dwell on such dead themes, not as one who
　　　　remembers,
　　But rather as one who sees.

She seemed one left behind of a band gone distant
　　So far that no tongue could hail:
Past things retold were to her as things existent,
　　Things present but as a tale.

May 20, 1902.

A CHURCH ROMANCE
(Mellstock: circa 1835)

She* turned in the high pew, until her sight
Swept the west gallery, and caught its row
Of music-men with viol, book, and bow
Against the sinking sad tower-window light.

She turned again; and in her pride's despite
One strenuous viol's inspirer seemed to throw
A message from his string to her below,
Which said: "I claim thee as my own forthright!"

Thus their hearts' bond began, in due time signed.
And long years thence, when Age had scared Romance,
At some old attitude of his or glance
That gallery-scene would break upon her mind,
With him as minstrel, ardent, young, and trim,
Bowing "New Sabbath" or "Mount Ephraim."**

---

* Hardy's mother.
** "New Sabbath" and "Mount Ephraim" are hymn tunes.

ON ONE WHO LIVED AND
DIED WHERE HE WAS BORN*

When a night in November
  Blew forth its bleared airs
An infant descended
  His birth-chamber stairs
  For the very first time,
  At the still, midnight chime;
All unapprehended
  His mission, his aim.—
Thus, first, one November,
An infant descended
    The stairs.

On a night in November
  Of weariful cares,
A frail aged figure
  Ascended those stairs
  For the very last time:
  All gone his life's prime,
All vanished his vigour,
  And fine, forceful frame:
Thus, last, one November
Ascended that figure
    Upstairs.

---

* Hardy's father.

On those nights in November—
  Apart eighty years—
The babe and the bent one
  Who traversed those stairs
  From the early first time
  To the last feeble climb—
That fresh and that spent one—
  Were even the same:
Yea, who passed in November
As infant, as bent one,
    Those stairs.

Wise child of November!
  From birth to blanched hairs
Descending, ascending,
  Wealth-wantless, those stairs;
  Who saw quick in time
  As a vain pantomime
Life's tending, its ending,
  The worth of its fame.
Wise child of November,
Descending, ascending
    Those stairs!

THE ROMAN ROAD

The Roman Road runs straight and bare
As the pale parting-line in hair
Across the heath. And thoughtful men
Contrast its days of Now and Then,
And delve, and measure, and compare;

Visioning on the vacant air
Helmed legionaries, who proudly rear
The Eagle, as they pace again
                    The Roman Road.

But no tall brass-helmed legionnaire
Haunts it for me. Uprises there
A mother's* form upon my ken,
Guiding my infant steps, as when
We walked that ancient thoroughfare,
                    The Roman Road.

---

* Hardy's mother.

THE SELF-UNSEEING

Here is the ancient floor,
Footworn and hollowed and thin,
Here was the former door
Where the dead feet walked in.

She sat here in her chair,
Smiling into the fire;
He who played stood there,
Bowing it higher and higher.

Childlike, I danced in a dream;
Blessings emblazoned that day;
Everything glowed with a gleam;
Yet we were looking away!

GEOGRAPHICAL KNOWLEDGE

(A MEMORY OF CHRISTIANA C——)

Where Blackmoor was, the road that led
    To Bath, she could not show,
Nor point the sky that overspread
    Towns ten miles off or so.

But that Calcutta stood this way,
    Cape Horn there figured fell,
That here was Boston, here Bombay,
    She could declare full well.

Less known to her the track athwart
    Froom Mead or Yell'ham Wood
Than how to make some Austral port
    In seas of surly mood.

She saw the glint of Guinea's shore
    Behind the plum-tree nigh,
Heard old unruly Biscay's roar
    In the weir's purl hard by. . . .

"My son's a sailor, and he knows
    All seas and many lands,
And when he's home he points and shows
    Each country where it stands.

"He's now just there—by Gib's high rock—
    And when he gets, you see,
To Portsmouth here, behind the clock,
    Then he'll come back to me!"

TO LOUISA* IN THE LANE

Meet me again as at that time
   In the hollow of the lane;
I will not pass as in my prime
   I passed at each day's wane.
         —Ah, I remember!
   To do it you will have to see
Anew this sorry scene wherein you have ceased to be!

But I will welcome your aspen form
   As you gaze wondering round
And say with spectral frail alarm,
   "Why am I still here found?
         —Ah, I remember!
   It is through him with blitheful brow
Who did not love me then, but loves and draws me now!"

And I shall answer: "Sweet of eyes,
   Carry me with you, Dear,
To where you donned this spirit-guise;
   It's better there than here!"
         —Till I remember
   Such is a deed you cannot do:
Wait must I, till with flung-off flesh I follow you.

---

* A farmer's daughter with whom the sixteen-year-old Hardy fell
in love. This poem was written a few months before Hardy's
death.

TO LIZBIE BROWNE*

I
Dear Lizbie Browne,
Where are you now?
In sun, in rain?—
Or is your brow
Past joy, past pain,
Dear Lizbie Browne?

II
Sweet Lizbie Browne,
How you could smile,
How you could sing!—
How archly wile
In glance-giving,
Sweet Lizbie Browne!

III
And, Lizbie Browne,
Who else had hair
Bay-red as yours,
Or flesh so fair
Bred out of doors,
Sweet Lizbie Browne?

IV
When, Lizbie Browne,
You had just begun
To be endeared
By stealth to one,
You disappeared,
My Lizbie Browne!

---

* The game-keeper's daughter.
At sixteen, Hardy loved her too.

V

Ay, Lizbie Browne,
So swift your life,
And mine so slow,
You were a wife
Ere I could show
Love, Lizbie Browne.

VI

Still, Lizbie Browne,
You won, they said,
The best of men
When you were wed. . . .
Where went you then,
O Lizbie Browne?

VII

Dear Lizbie Browne,
I should have thought,
"Girls ripen fast,"
And coaxed and caught
You ere you passed,
Dear Lizbie Browne!

VIII

But, Lizbie Browne,
I let you slip;
Shaped not a sign;
Touched never your lip
With lip of mine,
Lost Lizbie Browne!

IX
So, Lizbie Browne,
When on a day
Men speak of me
As not, you'll say,
"And who was he?"—
Yes, Lizbie Browne!

THOUGHTS OF PHENA*

AT NEWS OF HER DEATH

Not a line of her writing have I,
    Not a thread of her hair,
No mark of her late time as dame in her dwelling, whereby
    I may picture her there;
    And in vain do I urge my unsight
      To conceive my lost prize
At her close, whom I knew when her dreams were upbrim-
      ming with light,
    And with laughter her eyes.

What scenes spread around her last days,
    Sad, shining, or dim?
Did her gifts and compassions enray and enarch her sweet ways
    With an aureate nimb?
    Or did life-light decline from her years,
      And mischances control
Her full day-star; unease, or regret, or forebodings, or fears
    Disennoble her soul?

Thus I do but the phantom retain
    Of the maiden of yore
As my relic; yet haply the best of her—fined in my brain
    It may be the more
    That no line of her writing have I,
      Nor a thread of her hair,
No mark of her late time as dame in her dwelling, whereby
    I may picture her there.

March 1890.

---

* His cousin, Tryphena Sparks.

THE LAST SIGNAL
(*Oct.* 11, 1886)

A MEMORY OF WILLIAM BARNES*

Silently I footed by an uphill road
  That led from my abode to a spot yew-boughed;
Yellowly the sun sloped low down to westward,
    And dark was the east with cloud.

Then, amid the shadow of that livid sad east,
  Where the light was least, and a gate stood wide,
Something flashed the fire of the sun that was facing it,
    Like a brief blaze on that side.

Looking hard and harder I knew what it meant—
  The sudden shine sent from the livid east scene;
It meant the west mirrored by the coffin of my friend there,
    Turning to the road from his green,

To take his last journey forth—he who in his prime
  Trudged so many a time from that gate athwart the land!
Thus a farewell to me he signalled on his grave-way,
    As with a wave of his hand.

Winterborne-Came Path.

---

* A close friend. He was a clergyman and poet whose poems in the Dorset dialect were edited by Hardy.

In Time of the
Breaking of Nations
MEN AND WOMEN

IN TIME OF "THE BREAKING OF NATIONS"*

I

Only a man harrowing clods
   In a slow silent walk
With an old horse that stumbles and nods
   Half asleep as they stalk.

II

Only thin smoke without flame
   From the heaps of couch-grass;
Yet this will go onward the same
   Though Dynasties pass.

III

Yonder a maid and her wight
   Come whispering by:
War's annals will fade into night
   Ere their story die.

1915.

---

* *Jer. 51:20.*

THE MAN HE KILLED

"Had he and I but met
By some old ancient inn,
We should have sat us down to wet
Right many a nipperkin!

"But ranged as infantry,
And staring face to face,
I shot at him as he at me,
And killed him in his place.

"I shot him dead because—
Because he was my foe,
Just so: my foe of course he was;
That's clear enough; although

"He thought he'd 'list, perhaps,
Off-hand like—just as I—
Was out of work—had sold his traps—
No other reason why.

"Yes; quaint and curious war is!
You shoot a fellow down
You'd treat if met where any bar is,
Or help to half-a-crown."

1902.

DRUMMER HODGE

I

They throw in Drummer Hodge, to rest
    Uncoffined—just as found:
His landmark is a kopje-crest
    That breaks the veldt around;
And foreign constellations west
    Each night above his mound.

II

Young Hodge the Drummer never knew—
    Fresh from his Wessex home—
The meaning of the broad Karoo,
    The Bush, the dusty loam,
And why uprose in nightly view
    Strange stars amid the gloam.

III

Yet portion of that unknown plain
    Will Hodge for ever be;
His homely Northern breast and brain
    Grow to some Southern tree,
And strange-eyed constellations reign
    His stars eternally.

In the Boer War.

ON THE DEATH-BED

"I'll tell—being past all praying for—
Then promptly die . . . He was out at the war.
And got some scent of the intimacy
That was under way between her and me;
And he stole back home, and appeared like a ghost
One night, at the very time almost
That I reached her house. Well, I shot him dead,
And secretly buried him. Nothing was said.

"The news of the battle came next day;
He was scheduled missing. I hurried away,
Got out there, visited the field,
And sent home word that a search revealed
He was one of the slain; though, lying alone
And stript, his body had not been known.

"But she suspected. I lost her love,
Yea, my hope of earth, and of Heaven above;
And my time's now come, and I'll pay the score,
Though it be burning for evermore."

THE SERGEANT'S SONG
(1803)

When Lawyers strive to heal a breach,
And Parsons practise what they preach;
Then Boney* he'll come pouncing down,
And march his men on London town!
  Rollicum-rorum, tol-lol-lorum,
  Rollicum-rorum, tol-lol-lay!

When Justices hold equal scales,
And Rogues are only found in jails;
Then Boney he'll come pouncing down,
And march his men on London town!
  Rollicum-rorum, &c.

When Rich Men find their wealth a curse,
And fill therewith the Poor Man's purse;
Then Boney he'll come pouncing down,
And march his men on London town!
  Rollicum-rorum, &c.

When Husbands with their Wives agree,
And Maids won't wed from modesty;
Then Boney he'll come pouncing down,
And march his men on London town!
  Rollicum-rorum, tol-tol-lorum,
  Rollicum-rorum, tol-lol-lay!

1878.
Published in "The Trumpet-Major" 1880.

---

* Napoleon.

MAD SOLDIER'S SONG

I

Ha, for the snow and hoar!
Ho, for our fortune's made!
We can shape our bed without sheets to spread,
And our graves without a spade.
So foolish Life adieu
And ingrate Leader* too.
—Ah, but we loved you true!
Yet—he-he-he! and ho-ho-ho!—
We'll never return to you.

II

What can we wish for more?
Thanks to the frost and flood
We are grinning crones—thin bags of bones
Who once were flesh and blood.
So foolish Life adieu,
And ingrate Leader too.
—Ah, but we loved you true!
Yet—he-he-he! and ho-ho-ho!—
We'll never return to you.

Exhausted, they again crouch round the fire. Officers and privates press together for warmth. Other stragglers arrive, and sit at the backs of the first. With the progress of the night the stars come out in unusual brilliancy, Sirius and those in Orion flashing like stilettos; and the frost stiffens.

The fire sinks and goes out; but the Frenchmen do not move. The day dawns, and still they sit on.

In the background enter some light horse of the Russian army, followed by KUTÚZOF himself and a few of his staff. He presents a terrible appearance now—bravely serving though

---

* Napoleon.

44

slowly dying, his face puffed with the intense cold, his one eye staring out as he sits in a heap in the saddle, his head sunk into his shoulders. The whole detachment pauses at the sight of the French asleep. They shout; but the bivouackers give no sign.

KUTÚZOF
Go, stir them up! We slay not sleeping men.

The Russians advance and prod the French with their lances.

RUSSIAN OFFICER
Prince, here's a curious picture. They are dead.

KUTÚZOF (with indifference)
Oh, naturally. After the snow was down
I marked a sharpening of the air last night.
We shall be stumbling on such frost-baked meats
Most of the way to Wilna.

OFFICER (examining the bodies)
They all sit
As they were living still, but stiff as horns;
And even the colour has not left their cheeks,
Whereon the tears remain in strings of ice.—
It was a marvel they were not consumed:
Their clothes are cindered by the fire in front,
While at their back the frost has caked them hard.

KUTÚZOF
'Tis well. So perish Russia's enemies!

Exeunt KUTÚZOF, his staff, and the detachment of horse in the direction of Wilna; and with the advance of day the snow resumes its fall, slowly burying the dead bivouackers.

The French retreat from Moscow. From *The Dynasts*.

JEZREEL*

ON ITS SEIZURE BY THE ENGLISH UNDER ALLENBY,
SEPTEMBER 1918

Did they catch as it were in a Vision at shut of the day—
When their cavalry smote through the ancient Esdraelon Plain,
And they crossed where the Tishbite stood forth in his enemy's
    way—
His gaunt mournful Shade as he bade the King haste off amain?

On war-men at this end of time—even on Englishmen's eyes—
Who slay with their arms of new might in that long-ago place,
Flashed he who drove furiously? ... Ah, did the phantom arise
Of that queen, of the proud Tyrian woman who painted her
    face?

Faintly marked they the words "Throw her down!" rise from
    Night eerily,
Spectre-spots of the blood of her body on some rotten wall?
And the thin note of pity that came: "A King's daughter is she,"
As they passed where she trodden was once by the chargers'
    footfall?

Could such be the hauntings of men of to-day, at the cease
Of pursuit, at the dusk-hour, ere slumber their senses could seal?
Enghosted seers, kings—one on horseback who asked "Is it
    peace?"...
Yea, strange things and spectral may men have beheld in Jezreel!

September 24, 1918.

---

* The city where Jezebel was devoured by dogs. II Kings 9:30-36.

THE STRANGER'S SONG

(*As sung by* MR. CHARLES CHARRINGTON *in the play of*
"*The Three Wayfarers*")

O my trade it is the rarest one,
    Simple shepherds all—
  My trade is a sight to see;
For my customers I tie, and take 'em up on high,
  And waft 'em to a far countree!

My tools are but common ones,
    Simple shepherds all—
  My tools are no sight to see:
A little hempen string, and a post whereon to swing,
  Are implements enough for me!

To-morrow is my working day,
    Simple shepherds all—
  To-morrow is a working day for me:
For the farmer's sheep is slain, and the lad who did it ta'en,
  And on his soul may God ha' mer-cy!

Printed in "The Three Strangers," 1883.

THE LEVELLED CHURCHYARD

"O Passenger, pray list and catch
      Our sighs and piteous groans,
Half stifled in this jumbled patch
      Of wrenched memorial stones!

"We late-lamented, resting here,
      Are mixed to human jam,
And each to each exclaims in fear,
      'I know not which I am!'

"The wicked people have annexed
      The verses on the good;
A roaring drunkard sports the text
      Teetotal Tommy should!

"Where we are huddled none can trace,
      And if our names remain,
They pave some path or porch or place
      Where we have never lain!

"Here's not a modest maiden elf
      But dreads the final Trumpet,
Lest half of her should rise herself,
      And half some sturdy strumpet!

"From restorations of Thy fane,
      From smoothings of Thy sward,
From zealous Churchmen's pick and plane
      Deliver us O Lord! Amen!"

1882.

BY HER AUNT'S GRAVE

"Sixpence a week," says the girl to her lover,
"Aunt used to bring me, for she could confide
In me alone, she vowed. 'Twas to cover
The cost of her headstone when she died.
And that was a year ago last June;
I've not yet fixed it. But I must soon."

"And where is the money now, my dear?"
"O, snug in my purse . . . Aunt was *so* slow
In saving it—eighty weeks, or near.". . .
"Let's spend it," he hints. "For she won't know.
There's a dance to-night at the Load of Hay."
She passively nods. And they go that way.

SEEN BY THE WAITS

Through snowy woods and shady
    We went to play a tune
To the lonely manor-lady
    By the light of the Christmas moon.

We violed till, upward glancing
    To where a mirror leaned,
It showed her airily dancing,
    Deeming her movements screened;

Dancing alone in the room there,
    Thin-draped in her robe of night;
Her postures, glassed in the gloom there,
    Were a strange phantasmal sight.

She had learnt (we heard when homing)
    That her roving spouse was dead:
Why she had danced in the gloaming
    We thought, but never said.

SHE

AT HIS FUNERAL

They bear him to his resting-place—
In slow procession sweeping by;
I follow at a stranger's space;
His kindred they, his sweetheart I.
Unchanged my gown of garish dye,
Though sable-sad is their attire;
But they stand round with griefless eye,
Whilst my regret consumes like fire!

187-.

MIDNIGHT ON THE GREAT WESTERN

In the third-class seat sat the journeying boy,
    And the roof-lamp's oily flame
Played down on his listless form and face,
Bewrapt past knowing to what he was going,
    Or whence he came.

In the band of his hat the journeying boy
    Had a ticket stuck; and a string
Around his neck bore the key of his box,
That twinkled gleams of the lamp's sad beams
    Like a living thing.

What past can be yours, O journeying boy
    Towards a world unknown,
Who calmly, as if incurious quite
On all at stake, can undertake
    This plunge alone?

Knows your soul a sphere, O journeying boy,
    Our rude realms far above,
Whence with spacious vision you mark and mete
This region of sin that you find you in,
    But are not of?

AT THE RAILWAY STATION, UPWAY

"There is not much that I can do,
  For I've no money that's quite my own!"
  Spoke up the pitying child—
A little boy with a violin
At the station before the train came in,—
"But I can play my fiddle to you,
And a nice one 'tis, and good in tone!"

  The man in the handcuffs smiled;
The constable looked, and he smiled, too,
  As the fiddle began to twang;
And the man in the handcuffs suddenly sang
      With grimful glee:
     "This life so free
     Is the thing for me!"
And the constable smiled, and said no word,
As if unconscious of what he heard;
And so they went on till the train came in—
The convict, and boy with the violin.

THE HUSBAND'S VIEW

"Can anything avail
Beldame, for my hid grief?—
Listen: I'll tell the tale,
It may bring faint relief!—

"I came where I was not known,
In hope to flee my sin;
And walking forth alone
A young man said, 'Good e'en.'

"In gentle voice and true
He asked to marry me;
'You only—only you
Fulfil my dream!' said he.

"We married o' Monday morn,
In the month of hay and flowers;
My cares were nigh forsworn,
And perfect love was ours.

"But ere the days are long
Untimely fruit will show;
My Love keeps up his song,
Undreaming it is so.

"And I awake in the night,
And think of months gone by,
And of that cause of flight
Hidden from my Love's eye.

"Discovery borders near,
And then! . . . But something stirred?—
My husband—he is here!
Heaven—has he overheard?"—

"Yes; I have heard, sweet Nan;
I have known it all the time.
I am not a particular man;
Misfortunes are no crime:

"And what with our serious need
Of sons for soldiering,
That accident, indeed,
To maids, is a useful thing!"

THE RIVAL

I determined to find out whose it was—
   The portrait he looked at so, and sighed;
Bitterly have I rued my meanness
     And wept for it since he died!

I searched his desk when he was away,
   And there was the likeness—yes, my own!
Taken when I was the season's fairest,
     And time-lines all unknown.

I smiled at my image, and put it back,
   And he went on cherishing it, until
I was chafed that he loved not the me then living,
     But that past woman still.

Well, such was my jealousy at last,
   I destroyed that face of the former me;
Could you ever have dreamed the heart of woman
     Would work so foolishly!

THE RUINED MAID

"O 'Melia, my dear, this does everything crown!
Who could have supposed I should meet you in Town?
And whence such fair garments, such prosperi-ty?"—
"O didn't you know I'd been ruined?" said she.

—"You left us in tatters, without shoes or socks,
Tired of digging potatoes, and spudding up docks;
And now you've gay bracelets and bright feathers three!"—
"Yes: that's how we dress when we're ruined," said she.

—"At home in the barton you said 'thee' and 'thou,'
And 'thik oon,' and 'theäs oon,' and 't'other'; but now
Your talking quite fits 'ee for high compa-ny!"—
"Some polish is gained with one's ruin," said she.

—"Your hands were like paws then, your face blue and bleak
But now I'm bewitched by your delicate cheek,
And your little gloves fit as on any la-dy!"—
"We never do work when we're ruined," said she.

—"You used to call home-life a hag-ridden dream,
And you'd sigh, and you'd sock; but at present you seem
To know not of megrims or melancho-ly!"—
"True. One's pretty lively when ruined," said she.

—"I wish I had feathers, a fine sweeping gown,
And a delicate face, and could strut about Town!"—
"My dear—a raw country girl, such as you be,
Cannot quite expect that. You ain't ruined," said she.

Westbourne Park Villas, 1866.

THE WORKBOX

"See, here's the workbox, little wife,
   That I made of polished oak."
He was a joiner, of village life;
   She came of borough folk.

He holds the present up to her
   As with a smile she nears
And answers to the profferer,
   " 'Twill last all my sewing years!"

"I warrant it will. And longer too.
   'Tis a scantling that I got
Off poor John Wayward's coffin, who
   Died of they knew not what.

"The shingled pattern that seems to cease
   Against your box's rim
Continues right on in the piece
   That's underground with him.

"And while I worked it made me think
   Of timber's varied doom;
One inch where people eat and drink,
   The next inch in a tomb.

"But why do you look so white, my dear,
   And turn aside your face?
You knew not that good lad, I fear,
   Though he came from your native place?"

"How could I know that good young man,
    Though he came from my native town,
When he must have left far earlier than
    I was a woman grown?"

"Ah, no. I should have understood!
    It shocked you that I gave
To you one end of a piece of wood
    Whose other is in a grave?"

"Don't, dear, despise my intellect,
    Mere accidental things
Of that sort never have effect
    On my imaginings."

Yet still her lips were limp and wan,
    Her face still held aside,
As if she had known not only John,
    But known of what he died.

AT THE DRAPER'S

"I stood at the back of the shop, my dear,
   But you did not perceive me.
Well, when they deliver what you were shown
   I shall know nothing of it, believe me!"

And he coughed and coughed as she paled and said,
   "O, I didn't see you come in there—
Why couldn't you speak?"—"Well, I didn't. I left
   That you should not notice I'd been there.

"You were viewing some lovely things. '*Soon required
   For a widow, of latest fashion*';
And I knew 'twould upset you to meet the man
   Who had to be cold and ashen

"And screwed in a box before they could dress you
   '*In the last new note in mourning,*'
As they defined it. So, not to distress you,
   I left you to your adorning."

ROSE-ANN

Why didn't you say you was promised, Rose-Ann
 Why didn't you name it to me,
Ere ever you tempted me hither, Rose-Ann,
 So often, so wearifully?

O why did you let me be near 'ee, Rose-Ann,
 Talking things about wedlock so free,
And never by nod or by whisper, Rose-Ann,
 Give a hint that it wasn't to be?

Down home I was raising a flock of stock ewes,
 Cocks and hens, and wee chickens by scores,
And lavendered linen all ready to use,
 A-dreaming that they would be yours.

Mother said: "She's a sport-making maiden, my son";
 And a pretty sharp quarrel had we;
O why do you prove by this wrong you have done
 That I saw not what mother could see?

Never once did you say you was promised, Rose-Ann,
 Never once did I dream it to be;
And it cuts to the heart to be treated, Rose-Ann,
 As you in your scorning treat me!

THE CURATE'S KINDNESS
A Workhouse Irony

I

I thought they'd be strangers aroun' me,
    But she's to be there!
Let me jump out o' waggon and go back and drown me
    At Pummery or Ten-Hatches Weir.

II

I thought: "Well, I've come to the Union—
    The workhouse at last—
After honest hard work all the week, and Communion
    O' Zundays, these fifty years past.

III

" 'Tis hard; but," I thought, "never mind it:
    There's gain in the end:
And when I get used to the place I shall find it
    A home, and may find there a friend.

IV

"Life there will be better than t'other,
    For peace is assured.
The men in one wing and their wives in another
    Is strictly the rule of the Board."

V

Just then one young Pa'son arriving
    Steps up out of breath
To the side o' the waggon wherein we were driving
    To Union; and calls out and saith:

VI

"Old folks, that harsh order is altered,
 Be not sick of heart!
The Guardians they poohed and they pished and they paltered
 When urged not to keep you apart.

VII

" 'It is wrong,' I maintained, 'to divide them,
 Near forty years wed.'
'Very well, sir. We promise, then, they shall abide them
 In one wing together,' they said."

VIII

Then I sank—knew 'twas quite a foredone thing
 That misery should be
To the end! . . . To get freed of her there was the one thing
 Had made the change welcome to me.

IX

To go there was ending but badly;
 'Twas shame and 'twas pain;
"But anyhow," thought I, "thereby I shall gladly
 Get free of this forty years' chain."

X

I thought they'd be strangers aroun' me,
 But she's to be there!
Let me jump out o' waggon and go back and drown me
 At Pummery or Ten-Hatches Weir.

THE CHOIRMASTER'S BURIAL

He often would ask us
That, when he died,
After playing so many
To their last rest,
If out of us any
Should here abide,
And it would not task us,
We would with our lutes
Play over him
By his grave-brim
The psalm he liked best—
The one whose sense suits
"Mount Ephraim"*—
And perhaps we should seem
To him, in Death's dream,
Like the seraphim.

As soon as I knew
That his spirit was gone
I thought this his due,
And spoke thereupon.
"I think," said the vicar,
"A read service quicker
Than viols out-of-doors
In these frosts and hoars.
That old-fashioned way
Requires a fine day,
And it seems to me
It had better not be."

---

* A hymn tune.

Hence, that afternoon,
Though never knew he
That his wish could not be,
To get through it faster
They buried the master
Without any tune.

But 'twas said that, when
At the dead of next night
The vicar looked out,
There struck on his ken
Thronged roundabout,
Where the frost was graying
The headstoned grass,
A band all in white
Like the saints in church-glass,
Singing and playing
The ancient stave
By the choirmaster's grave.

Such the tenor man told
When he had grown old.

"AH, ARE YOU DIGGING ON
MY GRAVE?"

"Ah, are you digging on my grave
    My loved one?—planting rue?"
—"No: yesterday he went to wed
One of the brightest wealth has bred.
'It cannot hurt her now,' he said,
    'That I should not be true.' "

"Then who is digging on my grave?
    My nearest dearest kin?"
—"Ah, no: they sit and think, 'What use!
What good will planting flowers produce?
No tendance of her mound can loose
    Her spirit from Death's gin.' "

"But some one digs upon my grave?
    My enemy?—prodding sly?"
—"Nay: when she heard you had passed **the Gate**
That shuts on all flesh soon or late,
She thought you no more worth her **hate,**
    And cares not where you lie."

"Then, who is digging on my grave?
    Say—since I have not guessed!"
—"O it is I, my mistress dear,
Your little dog, who still lives near,
And much I hope my movements **here**
    Have not disturbed your rest?"

"Ah, yes! *You* dig upon my grave . . .
  Why flashed it not on me
That one true heart was left behind!
What feeling do we ever find
To equal among human kind
  A dog's fidelity!"

"Mistress, I dug upon your grave
  To bury a bone, in case
I should be hungry near this spot
When passing on my daily trot.
I am sorry, but I quite forgot
  It was your resting-place."

Hardy's only cynical view of the animal kingdom.

FARMER DUNMAN'S FUNERAL

"Bury me on a Sunday,"
    He said; "so as to see
Poor folk there. 'Tis their one day
    To spare for following me."

And mindful of that Sunday,
    He wrote, while he was well,
On ten rum-bottles one day,
    "Drink for my funeral."

They buried him on a Sunday,
    That folk should not be balked
His wish, as 'twas their one day:
    And forty couple walked.

They said: "To have it Sunday
    Was always his concern;
His meaning being that one day
    He'd do us a good turn.

"We must, had it been Monday,
    Have got it over soon.
But now we gain, being Sunday,
    A jolly afternoon."

NEUTRAL TONES

We stood by a pond that winter day,
And the sun was white, as though chidden of God,
And a few leaves lay on the starving sod;
    —They had fallen from an ash, and were gray.

Your eyes on me were as eyes that rove
Over tedious riddles of years ago;
And some words played between us to and fro
    On which lost the more by our love.

The smile on your mouth was the deadest thing
Alive enough to have strength to die;
And a grin of bitterness swept thereby
    Like an ominous bird a-wing. . . .

Since then, keen lessons that love deceives,
And wrings with wrong, have shaped to me
Your face, and the God-curst sun, and a tree,
    And a pond edged with grayish leaves.

1867.

IN THE ROOM OF THE BRIDE-ELECT

"Would it had been the man of our wish!"
Sighs her mother. To whom with vehemence she
In the wedding-dress—the wife to be—
"Then why were you so mollyish
As not to insist on him for me!"
The mother, amazed: "Why, dearest one,
Because you pleaded for this or none!"

"But Father and you should have stood out strong!
Since then, to my cost, I have lived to find
That you were right and that I was wrong;
This man is a dolt to the one declined. . . .
Ah!—here he comes with his button-hole rose.
Good God—I must marry him I suppose!"

MAD JUDY

When the hamlet hailed a birth
   Judy used to cry:
When she heard our christening mirth
   She would kneel and sigh.
She was crazed, we knew, and we
Humoured her infirmity.

When the daughters and the sons
   Gathered them to wed,
And we like-intending ones
   Danced till dawn was red,
She would rock and mutter, "More
Comers to this stony shore!"

When old Headsman Death laid hands
   On a babe or twain,
She would feast, and by her brands
Sing her songs again.
What she liked we let her do,
Judy was insane, we knew.

THE COLOUR

(The following lines are partly original, partly remembered from a Wessex folk-rhyme)

"What shall I bring you?
Please will white do
Best for your wearing
    The long day through?"
"—White is for weddings,
Weddings, weddings,
White is for weddings,
    And that won't do."

"What shall I bring you?
Please will red do
Best for your wearing
    The long day through?"
"—Red is for soldiers,
Soldiers, soldiers,
Red is for soldiers,
    And that won't do."

"What shall I bring you?
Please will blue do
Best for your wearing
    The long day through?"
"—Blue is for sailors,
Sailors, sailors,
Blue is for sailors,
    And that won't do."

"What shall I bring you?
Please will green do
Best for your wearing
    The long day through?"
"—Green is for mayings,
Mayings, mayings,
Green is for mayings,
    And that won't do."

"What shall I bring you
Then? Will black do
Best for your wearing
    The long day through?"
"—Black is for mourning,
Mourning, mourning,
Black is for mourning,
    And black will do."

JULIE-JANE

Sing; how 'a would sing!
How 'a would raise the tune
When we rode in the waggon from harvesting
    By the light o' the moon!

Dance; how 'a would dance!
If a fiddlestring did but sound
She would hold out her coats, give a slanting glance,
    And go round and round.

Laugh; how 'a would laugh!
Her peony lips would part
As if none such a place for a lover to quaff
    At the deeps of a heart.

Julie, O girl of joy,
Soon, soon that lover he came.
Ah, yes; and gave thee a baby-boy,
    But never his name. . . .

—Tolling for her, as you guess;
And the baby too. . . . 'Tis well.
You knew her in maidhood likewise?—Yes,
    That's her burial bell.

"I suppose," with a laugh, she said,
"I should blush that I'm not a wife;
But how can it matter, so soon to be dead,
    What one does in life!"

When we sat making the mourning
By her death-bed side, said she,
"Dears, how can you keep from your lovers, adorning
In honour of me!"

Bubbling and brightsome eyed!
But now—O never again.
She chose her bearers before she died
From her fancy-men.

*Note.—It is, or was, a common custom in Wessex, and
probably other country places, to prepare the mourning be-
side the death-bed, the dying person sometimes assisting, who
also selects his or her bearers on such occasions.*
"Coats" (line 7), old name for petticoats.

AFTER THE FAIR

The singers are gone from the Cornmarket-place
　　With their broadsheets of rhymes,
The street rings no longer in treble and bass
　　With their skits on the times,
And the Cross, lately thronged, is a dim naked space
　　That but echoes the stammering chimes.

From Clock-corner steps, as each quarter ding-dongs,
　　Away the folk roam
By the "Hart" and Grey's Bridge into byways and "drongs,"*
　　Or across the ridged loam;
The younger ones shrilling the lately heard songs,
　　The old saying, "Would we were home."

The shy-seeming maiden so mute in the fair
　　Now rattles and talks,
And that one who looked the most swaggering there
　　Grows sad as she walks,
And she who seemed eaten by cankering care
　　In statuesque sturdiness stalks.

And midnight clears High Street of all but the ghosts
　　Of its buried burghees,
From the latest far back to those old Roman hosts
　　Whose remains one yet sees,
Who loved, laughed, and fought, hailed their friends, drank
　　　their toasts
　　At their meeting-times here, just as these!

1902.

Note.—*"The Chimes" (line 6) will be listened for in vain here at mid-
night now, having been abolished some years ago.*

* Drong: a narrow passage (dialect).

THE PAT OF BUTTER

Once, at the Agricultural Show,
　　We tasted—all so yellow—
　　Those butter-pats, cool and mellow!
Each taste I still remember, though
　　It was so long ago.

This spoke of the grass of Netherhay,
　　And this of Kingcomb Hill,
　　And this of Coker Rill:
Which was the prime I could not say
　　Of all those tried that day.

Till she, the fair and wicked-eyed,
　　Held out a pat to me:
　　Then felt I all Yeo-Lea
Was by her sample sheer outvied;
　　And, "This is the best," I cried.

GREAT THINGS

Sweet cyder is a great thing,
　　A great thing to me,
Spinning down to Weymouth town
　　By Ridgway thirstily,
And maid and mistress summoning
　　Who tend the hostelry:
O cyder is a great thing,
　　A great thing to me!

The dance it is a great thing,
　　A great thing to me,
With candles lit and partners fit
　　For night-long revelry;
And going home when day-dawning
　　Peeps pale upon the lea:
O dancing is a great thing,
　　A great thing to me!

Love is, yea, a great thing,
　　A great thing to me,
When, having drawn across the lawn
　　In darkness silently,
A figure flits like one a-wing
　　Out from the nearest tree:
O love is, yes, a great thing,
　　A great thing to me!

Will these be always great things,
　　Great things to me? . . .
Let it befall that One will call,
　　"Soul, I have need of thee":
What then? Joy-jaunts, impassioned flings,
　　Love, and its ectasy,
Will always have been great things,
　　Great things to me!

The Spinner of the Years
MAN AND THE UNIVERSE

A DRIZZLING EASTER MORNING

And he is risen? Well, be it so....
And still the pensive lands complain,
And dead men wait as long ago,
As if, much doubting, they would know
What they are ransomed from, before
They pass again their sheltering door.

I stand amid them in the rain,
While blusters vex the yew and vane;
And on the road the weary wain
Plods forward, laden heavily;
And toilers with their aches are fain
For endless rest—though risen is he.

GOD-FORGOTTEN

I towered far, and lo! I stood within
The presence of the Lord Most High,
Sent thither by the sons of Earth, to win
    Some answer to their cry.

—"The Earth, sayest thou? The Human race?
By Me created? Sad its lot?
Nay: I have no remembrance of such place:
    Such world I fashioned not."—

—"O Lord, forgive me when I say
Thou spakest the word that made it all."—
"The Earth of men—let me bethink me. . . . Yea!
    I dimly do recall

"Some tiny sphere I built long back
(Mid millions of such shapes of mine)
So named . . . It perished, surely—not a wrack
    Remaining, or a sign?

"It lost my interest from the first,
My aims therefor succeeding ill;
Haply it died of doing as it durst?"—
    "Lord, it existeth still."—

"Dark, then, its life! For not a cry
Of aught it bears do I now hear;
Of its own act the threads were snapt whereby
    Its plaints had reached mine ear.

"It used to ask for gifts of good,
 Till came its severance, self-entailed,
When sudden silence on that side ensued,
        And has till now prevailed.

"All other orbs have kept in touch;
 Their voicings reach me speedily:
Thy people took upon them overmuch
        In sundering them from me!

"And it is strange—though sad enough—
 Earth's race should think that one whose call
Frames, daily, shining spheres of flawless stuff
        Must heed their tainted ball! . . .

"But sayest it is by pangs distraught,
 And strife, and silent suffering?—
Sore grieved am I that injury should be wrought
        Even on so poor a thing!

"Thou shouldst have learnt that *Not to Mend*
 For Me could mean but *Not to Know:*
Hence, Messengers! and straightway put an end
        To what men undergo.". .

Homing at dawn, I thought to see
 One of the Messengers standing by.
—Oh, childish thought! . . . Yet often it comes to me
        When trouble hovers nigh.

BY THE EARTH'S CORPSE

I

"O Lord, why grievest Thou?—
    Since Life has ceased to be
Upon this globe, now cold
    As lunar land and sea,
And humankind, and fowl, and fur
    Are gone eternally,
All is the same to Thee as ere
    They knew mortality."

II

"O Time," replied the Lord,
    "Thou readest me ill, I ween;
Were all *the same,* I should not grieve
    At that late earthly scene,
Now blestly past—though planned by me
    With interest close and keen!—
Nay, nay: things now are *not* the same
    As they have earlier been.

III

    "Written indelibly
    On my eternal mind
    Are all the wrongs endured
    By Earth's poor patient kind,
Which my too oft unconscious hand
    Let enter undesigned.
No god can cancel deeds fordone,
    Or thy old coils unwind!

IV

"As when, in Noë's days,
I whelmed the plains with sea,
So at this last, when flesh
And herb but fossils be,
And, all extinct, their piteous dust
Revolves obliviously,
That I made Earth, and life, and man,
It still repenteth me!"

THE IMPERCIPIENT

(AT A CATHEDRAL SERVICE)

That with this bright believing band
    I have no claim to be,
That faiths by which my comrades stand
    Seem fantasies to me,
And mirage-mists their Shining Land,
    Is a strange destiny.

Why thus my soul should be consigned
    To infelicity,
Why always I must feel as blind
    To sights my brethren see,
Why joys they've found I cannot find,
    Abides a mystery.

Since heart of mine knows not that ease
    Which they know; since it be
That He who breathes All's Well to these
    Breathes no All's-Well to me,
My lack might move their sympathies
    And Christian charity!

I am like a gazer who should mark
    An inland company
Standing upfingered, with, "Hark! hark!
    The glorious distant sea!"
And feel, "Alas, 'tis but yon dark
    And wind-swept pine to me!"

Yet I would bear my shortcomings
　　With meet tranquillity,
But for the charge that blessed things
　　I'd liefer not have be.
O, doth a bird deprived of wings
　　Go earth-bound wilfully!
　　·　　·　　·　　·　　·

Enough. As yet disquiet clings
　　About us. Rest shall we.

THOUGHTS AT MIDNIGHT

Mankind, you dismay me
When shadows waylay me!—
Not by your splendours
Do you affray me,
Not as pretenders
To demonic keenness,
Not by your meanness,
Nor your ill-teachings,
Nor your false preachings,
Nor your banalities
And immoralities,
Nor by your daring
Nor sinister bearing;
But by your madnesses
Capping cool badnesses,
Acting like puppets
Under Time's buffets;
In superstitions
And ambitions
Moved by no wisdom,
Far-sight, or system,
Led by sheer senselessness
And presciencelessness
Into unreason
And hideous self-treason. . . .
God, look he on you,
Have mercy upon you!

Part written 25th May 1906.

SURVIEW*
"Cogitavi vias meas"**

A cry from the green-grained sticks of the fire
    Made me gaze where it seemed to be:
'Twas my own voice talking therefrom to me
Oh how I had walked when my sun was higher—
    My heart in its arrogancy.

"You held not to whatsoever was true,"
    Said my own voice talking to me:
*"Whatsoever was just you were slack to see;
Kept not things lovely and pure in view,"*
    Said my own voice talking to me.

"You slighted her that endureth all,"
    Said my own voice talking to me;
*"Vaunteth not, trusteth hopefully;
That suffereth long and is kind withal,"*
    Said my own voice talking to me.

"You taught not that which you set about,"
    Said my own voice talking to me:
"That the greatest of things is Charity. . . ."
—And the sticks burnt low, and the fire went out,
    And my voice ceased talking to me.

---

* An archaic word meaning "Survey." It was also used
by Browning.
** "I have considered my ways."

"I TRAVEL AS A PHANTOM NOW"

I travel as a phantom now,
For people do not wish to see
In flesh and blood so bare a bough
    As Nature makes of me.

And thus I visit bodiless
Strange gloomy households often at odds,
And wonder if Man's consciousness
    Was a mistake of God's.

And next I meet you, and I pause,
And think that if mistake it were,
As some have said, O then it was
    One that I well can bear!

1915.

THE OXEN

Christmas Eve, and twelve of the clock.
   "Now they are all on their knees,"
An elder said as we sat in a flock
   By the embers in hearthside ease.

We pictured the meek mild creatures where
   They dwelt in their strawy pen,
Nor did it occur to one of us there
   To doubt they were kneeling then.

So fair a fancy few would weave
   In these years! Yet, I feel,
If someone said on Christmas Eve,
   "Come; see the oxen kneel,

"In the lonely barton* by yonder coomb
   Our childhood used to know,"
I should go with him in the gloom,
   Hoping it might be so.

1915.

---

* Farm.

YULETIDE IN A YOUNGER WORLD

We believed in highdays then,
    And could glimpse at night
      On Christmas Eve
Imminent oncomings of radiant revel—
    Doings of delight:—
    Now we have no such sight.

We had eyes for phantoms then,
    And at bridge or stile
      On Christmas Eve
Clear beheld those countless ones who had crossed it
    Cross again in file:—
    Such has ceased longwhile!

We liked divination then,
    And, as they homeward wound
      On Christmas Eve,
We could read men's dreams within them spinning
    Even as wheels spin round:—
    Now we are blinker-bound.

We heard still small voices then,
    And, in the dim serene
      Of Christmas Eve,
Caught the fartime tones of fire-filled prophets
    Long on earth unseen. . . .
    —Can such ever have been?

CHRISTMAS: 1924

"Peace upon earth!" was said. We sing it,
And pay a million priests to bring it.
After two thousand years of mass
We've got as far as poison-gas.

1924.

MUTE OPINION

I

I traversed a dominion
Whose spokesmen spake out strong
Their purpose and opinion
Through pulpit, press, and song.
I scarce had means to note there
A large-eyed few, and dumb,
Who thought not as those thought there
That stirred the heat and hum.

II

When, grown a Shade, beholding
That land in lifetime trode,
To learn if its unfolding
Fulfilled its clamoured code,
I saw, in web unbroken,
Its history outwrought
Not as the loud had spoken,
But as the mute had thought.

A YOUNG MAN'S EPIGRAM
ON EXISTENCE

A senseless school, where we must give
Our lives that we may learn to live!
A dolt is he who memorizes
Lessons that leave no time for prizes.

1866.

Hardy called this "an amusing instance of
early cynicism."

THE CONVERGENCE OF THE TWAIN

(Lines on the loss of the "Titanic")

I

In a solitude of the sea
Deep from human vanity,
And the Pride of Life that planned her, stilly couches she.

II

Steel chambers, late the pyres
Of her salamandrine fires,
Cold currents thrid, and turn to rhythmic tidal lyres.

III

Over the mirrors meant
To glass the opulent
The sea-worm crawls—grotesque, slimed, dumb, indifferent.

IV

Jewels in joy designed
To ravish the sensuous mind
Lie lightless, all their sparkles bleared and black and blind.

V

Dim moon-eyed fishes near
Gaze at the gilded gear
And query: "What does this vaingloriousness down here?". . .

VI

Well: while was fashioning
This creature of cleaving wing,
The Immanent Will that stirs and urges everything

VII

Prepared a sinister mate
For her—so gaily great—
A Shape of Ice, for the time far and dissociate.

VIII

And as the smart ship grew
In stature, grace, and hue,
In shadowy silent distance grew the Iceberg too.

IX

Alien they seemed to be:
No mortal eye could see
The intimate welding of their later history.

X

Or sign that they were bent
By paths coincident
On being anon twin halves of one august event.

XI

Till the Spinner of the Years
Said "Now!" And each one hears,
And consummation comes, and jars two hemispheres.

A NECESSITARIAN'S EPITAPH

A world I did not wish to enter
Took me and poised me on my centre,
Made me grimace, and foot, and prance,
As cats on hot bricks have to dance
Strange jigs to keep them from the floor,
Till they sink down and feel no more.

HAP

If but some vengeful god would call to me
From up the sky, and laugh: "Thou suffering thing,
Know that thy sorrow is my ecstasy,
That thy love's loss is my hate's profiting!"

Then would I bear it, clench myself, and die,
Steeled by the sense of ire unmerited;
Half-eased in that a Powerfuller than I
Had willed and meted me the tears I shed.

But not so. How arrives it joy lies slain,
And why unblooms the best hope ever sown?
—Crass Casualty obstructs the sun and rain,
And dicing Time for gladness casts a moan . . .
These purblind Doomsters had as readily strown
Blisses about my pilgrimage as pain.

1866.

WAITING BOTH

A star looks down at me,
And says: "Here I and you
Stand, each in our degree;
What do you mean to do,—
    Mean to do?"

I say: "For all I know,
Wait, and let Time go by,
Till my change come."—"Just so."
The star says: "So mean I:—
    So mean I."

When I Set Out for Lyonnesse
LOVE AND MARRIAGE

"WHEN I SET OUT FOR LYONNESSE"*
(1870)

When I set out for Lyonnesse,
   A hundred miles away,
   The rime was on the spray,
And starlight lit my lonesomeness
When I set out for Lyonnesse
   A hundred miles away.

What would bechance at Lyonnesse
   While I should sojourn there
   No prophet durst declare,
Nor did the wisest wizard guess
What would bechance at Lyonnesse
   While I should sojourn there.

When I came back from Lyonnesse
   With magic in my eyes,
   All marked with mute surmise
My radiance rare and fathomless,
When I came back from Lyonnesse
   With magic in my eyes!

---

* Lyonnesse was Hardy's name for
Cornwall. In Arthurian legend it was
contiguous to Cornwall.

FIRST SIGHT OF HER
AND AFTER

A day is drawing to its fall
   I had not dreamed to see;
The first of many to enthrall
   My spirit, will it be?
Or is this eve the end of all
   Such new delight for me?

I journey home: the pattern grows
   Of moonshades on the way:
"Soon the first quarter, I suppose,"
   Sky-glancing travellers say;
I realize that it, for those,
   Has been a common day.

"A MAN WAS DRAWING NEAR TO ME"

On that gray night of mournful drone,
Apart from aught to hear, to see,
I dreamt not that from shires unknown
     In gloom, alone,
     By Halworthy,
A man was drawing near to me.

I'd no concern at anything,
No sense of coming pull-heart play;
Yet, under the silent outspreading
     Of even's wing
     Where Otterham lay,
A man was riding up my way.

I thought of nobody—not of one,
But only of trifles—legends, ghosts—
Though, on the moorland dim and dun
     That travellers shun
     About these coasts,
The man had passed Tresparret Posts.

There was no light at all inland,
Only the seaward pharos-fire,
Nothing to let me understand
     That hard at hand
     By Hennett Byre
The man was getting nigh and nigher.

There was a rumble at the door,
A draught disturbed the drapery,
And but a minute passed before,
     With gaze that bore
     My destiny,
The man revealed himself to me.

AT THE WORD "FAREWELL"

She looked like a bird from a cloud
    On the clammy lawn,
Moving alone, bare-browed
    In the dim of dawn.
The candles alight in the room
    For my parting meal
Made all things withoutdoors loom
    Strange, ghostly, unreal.

The hour itself was a ghost,
    And it seemed to me then
As of chances the chance furthermost
    I should see her again.
I beheld not where all was so fleet
    That a Plan of the past
Which had ruled us from birthtime to meet
    Was in working at last:

No prelude did I there perceive
    To a drama at all,
Or foreshadow what fortune might weave
    From beginnings so small;
But I rose as if quicked by a spur
    I was bound to obey,
And stepped through the casement to her
    Still alone in the gray.

"I am leaving you. . . . Farewell!" I said,
  As I followed her on
By an alley bare boughs overspread;
  "I soon must be gone!"
Even then the scale might have been turned
  Against love by a feather,
—But crimson one cheek of hers burned
  When we came in together.

OVERLOOKING THE RIVER STOUR*

The swallows flew in the curves of an eight
    Above the river-gleam
Like little crossbows animate
The swallows flew in the curves of an eight
    Above the river-gleam.

Planing up shavings of crystal spray
    A moor-hen darted out
    From the bank thereabout,
And through the stream-shine ripped his way;
Planing up shavings of crystal spray
    A moor-hen darted out.

Closed were the kingcups; and the mead
    Dripped in monotonous green,
    Though the day's morning sheen
Had shown it golden and honeybee'd;
Closed were the kingcups; and the mead
    Dripped in monotonous green.

And never I turned my head, alack,
    While these things met my gaze
    Through the pane's drop-drenched glaze,
To see the more behind my back. . . .
O never I turned, but let, alack,
    These less things hold my gaze!

---

* Written in their first house at Sturminster Newton,
Dorset.

LOST LOVE

I play my sweet old airs—
  The airs he knew
  When our love was true—
  But he does not balk
  His determined walk,
And passes up the stairs.

I sing my songs once more,
  And presently hear
  His footstep near
  As if it would stay;
  But he goes his way,
And shuts a distant door.

So I wait for another morn,
  And another night
  In this soul-sick blight;
  And I wonder much
  As I sit, why such
A woman as I was born!

THE INTERLOPER

"And I saw the figure and visage of Madness
seeking for a home."

There are three folk driving in a quaint old chaise,
And the cliff-side track looks green and fair:
I view them talking in quiet glee
As they drop down towards the puffins' lair
      By the roughest of ways;
But another with the three rides on, I see,
      Whom I like not to be there!

No: it's not anybody you think of. Next
A dwelling appears by a slow sweet stream
Where two sit happy and half in the dark:
They read, helped out by a frail-wick'd gleam,
      Some rhythmic text;
But one sits with them whom they don't mark,
      One I'm wishing could not be there.

No: not whom you knew and name. And now
I discern gay diners in a mansion-place,
And the guests dropping wit—pert, prim, or choice,
And the hostess's tender and laughing face,
      And the host's bland brow;
But I cannot help hearing a hollow voice,
      And I'd fain not hear it there.

No: it's not from the stranger you met once. Ah,
Yet a goodlier scene than that succeeds;
People on a lawn—quite a crowd of them. Yes,
And they chatter and ramble as fancy leads;
      And they say, "Hurrah!"
To a blithe speech made; save one, mirthless,
      Who ought not to be there.

Nay: it's not the pale Form your imagings raise,
That waits on us all at a destined time,
It is not the Fourth Figure* the Furnace showed;
O that it were such a shape sublime
      In these latter days!
It is that under which best lives corrode;
      Would, would it could not be there!

---

* Daniel 3:25. This may refer to a possible mental break-
down of Emma's, as may also "The Man with a Past."

THE MAN WITH A PAST

There was merry-making
When the first dart fell
As a heralding,—
Till grinned the fully bared thing,
And froze like a spell—
Like a spell.

Innocent was she,
Innocent was I,
Too simple we!
Before us we did not see,
Nearing, aught wry—
Aught wry!

I can tell it not now,
It was long ago;
And such things cow;
But that is why and how
Two lives were so—
Were so.

Yes, the years matured,
And the blows were three
That time ensured
On her, which she dumbly endured;
And one on me—
One on me.

THE DIVISION

Rain on the windows, creaking doors,
 With blasts that besom the green,
And I am here, and you are there,
 And a hundred miles between!

O were it but the weather, Dear,
 O were it but the miles
That summed up all our severance,
 There might be room for smiles.

But that thwart thing betwixt us twain,
 Which nothing cleaves or clears,
Is more than distance, Dear, or rain,
 And longer than the years!

189–.

HAD YOU WEPT

Had you wept; had you but neared me with a hazed uncer-
tain ray,
Dewy as the face of the dawn, in your large and luminous eye,
Then would have come back all the joys the tidings had slain
that day,
And a new beginning, a fresh fair heaven, have smoothed the
things awry.
But you were less feebly human, and no passionate need for
clinging
Possessed your soul to overthrow reserve when I came near;
Ay, though you suffer as much as I from storms the hours are
bringing
Upon your heart and mine, I never see you shed a tear.

The deep strong woman is weakest, the weak one is the
strong;
The weapon of all weapons best for winning, you have not
used;
Have you never been able, or would you not, through the evil
times and long?
Has not the gift been given you, or such gift have you
refused?
When I bade me not absolve you on that evening or the
morrow,
Why did you not make war on me with those who weep like
rain?
You felt too much, so gained no balm for all your torrid
sorrow,
And hence our deep division, and our dark undying pain.

"YOU WERE THE SORT
THAT MEN FORGET"

You were the sort that men forget;
  Though I—not yet!—
Perhaps not ever. Your slighted weakness
  Adds to the strength of my regret!

You'd not the art—you never had
  For good or bad—
To make men see how sweet your meaning,
  Which, visible, had charmed them glad.

You would, by words inept let fall,
  Offend them all,
Even if they saw your warm devotion
  Would hold your life's blood at their call.

You lacked the eye to understand
  Those friends offhand
Whose mode was crude, though whose dim purport
  Outpriced the courtesies of the bland.

I am now the only being who
  Remembers you
It may be. What a waste that Nature
  Grudged soul so dear the art its due!

WITHOUT, NOT WITHIN HER

It was what you bore with you, Woman,
  Not inly were,
That throned you from all else human,
  However fair!

It was that strange freshness you carried
  Into a soul
Whereon no thought of yours tarried
  Two moments at all.

And out from his spirit flew death,
  And bale, and ban,
Like the corn-chaff under the breath
  Of the winnowing-fan.

LINES

Show me again the time
When in the Junetide's prime
We flew by meads and mountains northerly!—
Yea, to such freshness, fairness, fulness, fineness, freeness,
Love lures life on.

Show me again the day
When from the sandy bay
We looked together upon the pestered sea!—
Yea, to such surging, swaying, sighing, swelling, shrinking,
Love lures life on.

Show me again the hour
When by the pinnacled tower
We eyed each other and feared futurity!—
Yea, to such bodings, broodings, beatings, blanchings, blessings,
Love lures life on.

Show me again just this:
The moment of that kiss
Away from the prancing folk, by the strawberry-tree!—
Yea, to such rashness, ratheness, rareness, ripeness, richness,
Love lures life on.

Begun November 1898.

IN TENEBRIS*

"Percussus sum sicut foenum,
et aruit cor meum."** *Ps. ci.*

　　　Wintertime nighs;
But my bereavement-pain
It cannot bring again:
　　　Twice no one dies.

　　　Flower-petals flee;
But, since it once hath been,
No more that severing scene
　　　Can harrow me.

　　　Birds faint in dread:
I shall not lose old strength
In the lone frost's black length:
　　　Strength long since fled!

　　　Leaves freeze to dun;
But friends can not turn cold
This season as of old
　　　For him with none.

　　　Tempests may scath;
But love can not make smart
Again this year his heart
　　　Who no heart hath.

　　　Black is night's cope;
But death will not appal
One who, past doubtings all,
　　　Waits in unhope.

---

* In the shadows.
** "I am cut down like straw, and my heart withers."

WITHOUT CEREMONY

It was your way, my dear,
To vanish without a word
When callers, friends, or kin
Had left, and I hastened in
To rejoin you, as I inferred.

And when you'd a mind to career
Off anywhere—say to town—
You were all on a sudden gone
Before I had thought thereon,
Or noticed your trunks were down.

So, now that you disappear
For ever in that swift style,
Your meaning seems to me
Just as it used to be:
"Good-bye is not worth while."

1912.

THE HAUNTER

He does not think that I haunt here nightly:
　　How shall I let him know
That whither his fancy sets him wandering
　　I, too, alertly go?—
Hover and hover a few feet from him
　　Just as I used to do,
But cannot answer the words he lifts me—
　　Only listen thereto!

When I could answer he did not say them:
　　When I could let him know
How I would like to join in his journeys
　　Seldom he wished to go.
Now that he goes and wants me with him
　　More than he used to do,
Never he sees my faithful phantom
　　Though he speaks thereto.

Yes, I companion him to places
　　Only dreamers know,
Where the shy hares print long paces,
　　Where the night rooks go;
Into old aisles where the past is all to him,
　　Close as his shade can do,
Always lacking the power to call to him,
　　Near as I reach thereto!

What a good haunter I am, O tell him!
    Quickly make him know
If he but sigh since my loss befell him
    Straight to his side I go.
Tell him a faithful one is doing
    All that love can do
Still that his path may be worth pursuing,
    And to bring peace thereto.

1912.

HER SONG

I sang that song on Sunday,
  To witch an idle while,
I sang that song on Monday,
  As fittest to beguile:
I sang it as the year outwore,
    And the new slid in;
I thought not what might shape before
  Another would begin.

I sang that song in summer,
  All unforeknowingly,
To him as a new-comer
  From regions strange to me:
I sang it when in afteryears
    The shades stretched out,
And paths were faint; and flocking fears
  Brought cup-eyed care and doubt.

Sings he that song on Sundays
  In some dim land afar,
On Saturdays, or Mondays,
  As when the evening star
Glimpsed in upon his bending face,
    And my hanging hair,
And time untouched me with a trace
  Of soul-smart or despair?

AN UPBRAIDING

Now I am dead you sing to me
    The songs we used to know,
But while I lived you had no wish
    Or care for doing so.

Now I am dead you come to me
    In the moonlight, comfortless;
Ah, what would I have given alive
    To win such tenderness!

When you are dead, and stand to me
    Not differenced, as now,
But like again, will you be cold
    As when we lived, or how?

THE VOICE

Woman much missed, how you call to me, call to me,
Saying that now you are not as you were
When you had changed from the one who was all to me
But as at first, when our day was fair.

Can it be you that I hear? Let me view you, then,
Standing as when I draw near to the town
Where you would wait for me: yes, as I knew you then,
Even to the original air-blue gown!

Or is it only the breeze, in its listlessness
Travelling across the wet mead to me here,
You being ever dissolved to wan wistlessness,
Heard no more again far or near?

    Thus I; faltering forward,
    Leaves around me falling,
Wind oozing thin through the thorn from norward,
    And the woman calling.

December 1912.

A NIGHT IN NOVEMBER

I marked when the weather changed,
And the panes began to quake,
And the winds rose up and ranged,
That night, lying half-awake.

Dead leaves blew into my room,
And alighted upon my bed,
And a tree declared to the gloom
In sorrow that they were shed.

One leaf of them touched my hand,
And I thought that it was you
There stood as you used to stand,
And saying at last you knew!

(?) *1913.*

THE WALK

You did not walk with me
Of late to the hill-top tree
    By the gated ways,
    As in earlier days;
    You were weak and lame,
    So you never came,
And I went alone, and I did not mind,
Not thinking of you as left behind.

I walked up there to-day
Just in the former way;
    Surveyed around
    The familiar ground
    By myself again:
    What difference, then?
Only that underlying sense
Of the look of a room on returning thence.

THE FIGURE IN THE SCENE

It pleased her to step in front and sit
    Where the cragged slope was green,
While I stood back that I might pencil it
    With her amid the scene;
      Till it gloomed and rained;
But I kept on, despite the drifting wet
    That fell and stained
My draught, leaving for curious quizzings yet
    The blots engrained.

And thus I drew her there alone,
    Seated amid the gauze
Of moisture, hooded, only her outline shown,
    With rainfall marked across.
      —Soon passed our stay;
Yet her rainy form is the Genius still of the spot,
    Immutable, yea,
Though the place now knows her no more and has known her
        not
    Ever since that day.

From an old note.

AFTER A JOURNEY

Hereto I come to view a voiceless ghost;
   Whither, O whither will its whim now draw me?
Up the cliff, down, till I'm lonely, lost,
   And the unseen waters' ejaculations awe me.
Where you will next be there's no knowing,
   Facing round about me everywhere,
      With your nut-coloured hair,
And gray eyes, and rose-flush coming and going.

Yes: I have re-entered your olden haunts at last;
   Though the years, through the dead scenes I have
         tracked you;
What have you now found to say of our past—
   Scanned across the dark space wherein I have lacked you?
Summer gave us sweets, but autumn wrought division?
   Things were not lastly as firstly well
      With us twain, you tell?
But all's closed now, despite Time's derision.

I see what you are doing: you are leading me on
   To the spots we knew when we haunted here together,
The waterfall, above which the mist-bow shone
   At the then fair hour in the then fair weather,
And the cave just under, with a voice still so hollow
   That it seems to call out to me from forty years ago,
      When you were all aglow,
And not the thin ghost that I now frailly follow!

Ignorant of what there is flitting here to see,
    The waked birds preen and the seals flop lazily,
Soon you will have, Dear, to vanish from me,
    For the stars close their shutters and the dawn whitens hazily.
Trust me, I mind not, though Life lours,
    The bringing me here; nay, bring me here again!
        I am just the same as when
Our days were a joy, and our paths through flowers.

Pentargan Bay.

RAIN ON A GRAVE

Clouds spout upon her
  Their waters amain
  In ruthless disdain,—
Her who but lately
  Had shivered with pain
As at touch of dishonour
If there had lit on her
So coldly, so straightly
  Such arrows of rain:

One who to shelter
  Her delicate head
Would quicken and quicken
  Each tentative tread
If drops chanced to pelt her
  That summertime spills
  In dust-paven rills
When thunder-clouds thicken
  And birds close their bills.

Would that I lay there
  And she were housed here!
Or better, together
Were folded away there
Exposed to one weather
We both,—who would stray there
When sunny the day there,
  Or evening was clear
  At the prime of the year.

Soon will be growing
    Green blades from her mound,
And daisies be showing
    Like stars on the ground,
Till she form part of them—
Ay—the sweet heart of them,
Loved beyond measure
With a child's pleasure
    All her life's round.

Jan. 31, 1913.

A WOMAN DRIVING

How she held up the horses' heads,
　　Firm-lipped, with steady rein,
Down that grim steep the coastguard treads,
　　Till all was safe again!

With form erect and keen contour
　　She passed against the sea,
And, dipping into the chine's obscure,
　　Was seen no more by me.

To others she appeared anew
　　At times of dusky light,
But always, so they told, withdrew
　　From close and curious sight.

Some said her silent wheels would roll
　　Rutless on softest loam,
And even that her steeds' footfall
　　Sank not upon the foam.

Where drives she now? It may be where
　　No mortal horses are,
But in a chariot of the air
　　Towards some radiant star.

A DREAM OR NO

Why go to Saint-Juliot?* What's Juliot to me?
      Some strange necromancy
      But charmed me to fancy
That much of my life claims the spot as its key.

Yes. I have had dreams of that place in the West,
      And a maiden abiding
      Thereat as in hiding;
Fair-eyed and white-shouldered, broad-browed and
          brown-tressed.

And of how, coastward bound on a night long ago,
      There lonely I found her,
      The sea-birds around her,
And other than nigh things uncaring to know.

So sweet her life there (in my thought has it seemed)
      That quickly she drew me
      To take her unto me,
And lodge her long years with me. Such have I dreamed.

But nought of that maid from Saint-Juliot I see;
      Can she ever have been here,
      And shed her life's sheen here,
The woman I thought a long housemate with me?

Does there even a place like Saint-Juliot exist?
      Or a Vallency Valley
      With stream and leafed alley,
Or Beeny, or Bos with its flounce flinging mist?

February 1913.

---

* The town in Cornwall where Hardy met his wife Emma.

AT CASTLE BOTEREL

As I drive to the junction of lane and highway,
  And the drizzle bedrenches the waggonette,
I look behind at the fading byway,
  And see on its slope, now glistening wet,
    Distinctly yet

Myself and a girlish form benighted
  In dry March weather. We climb the road
Beside a chaise. We had just alighted
  To ease the sturdy pony's load
    When he sighed and slowed.

What we did as we climbed, and what we talked of
  Matters not much, nor to what it led,—
Something that life will not be balked of
  Without rude reason till hope is dead,
    And feeling fled.

It filled but a minute. But was there ever
  A time of such quality, since or before,
In that hill's story? To one mind never,
  Though it has been climbed, foot-swift, foot-sore,
    By thousands more.

Primaeval rocks form the road's steep border,
  And much have they faced there, first and last,
Of the transitory in Earth's long order;
  But what they record in colour and cast
    Is—that we two passed.

And to me, though Time's unflinching rigour,
  In mindless rote, has ruled from sight
The substance now, one phantom figure
  Remains on the slope, as when that night
    Saw us alight.

I look and see it there, shrinking, shrinking,
  I look back at it amid the rain
For the very last time; for my sand is sinking,
  And I shall traverse old love's domain
    Never again.

March 1913.

BEENY CLIFF

March 1870—*March* 1913

I

O the opal and the sapphire of that wandering western sea,
And the woman riding high above with bright hair flapping
    free—
The woman whom I loved so, and who loyally loved me.

II

The pale mews plained below us, and the waves seemed far
    away
In a nether sky, engrossed in saying their ceaseless babbling
    say,
As we laughed light-heartedly aloft on that clear-sunned March
    day.

III

A little cloud then cloaked us, and there flew an irised rain,
And the Atlantic dyed its levels with a dull misfeatured stain,
And then the sun burst out again, and purples prinked the main.

IV

—Still in all its chasmal beauty bulks old Beeny to the sky,
And shall she and I not go there once again now March is nigh,
And the sweet things said in that March say anew there by
    and by?

V

What if still in chasmal beauty looms that wild weird western
    shore,
The woman now is—elsewhere—whom the ambling pony bore,
And nor knows nor cares for Beeny, and will laugh there never-
    more.

"IT NEVER LOOKS LIKE SUMMER"

"It never looks like summer here
    On Beeny by the sea."
But though she saw its look as drear,
    Summer it seemed to me.

It never looks like summer now
    Whatever weather's there;
But ah, it cannot anyhow,
    On Beeny or elsewhere!

Boscastle.
March 8, 1913.

AFTER THE VISIT

(TO F. E. D.)*

Come again to the place
Where your presence was as a leaf that skims
Down a drouthy way whose ascent bedims
      The bloom on the farer's face.

Come again, with the feet
That were light on the green as a thistledown ball,
And those mute ministrations to one and to all
      Beyond a man's saying sweet.

Until then the faint scent
Of the bordering flowers swam unheeded away,
And I marked not the charm in the changes of day
      As the cloud-colours came and went.

Through the dark corridors
Your walk was so soundless I did not know
Your form from a phantom's of long ago
      Said to pass on the ancient floors,

Till you drew from the shade,
And I saw the large luminous living eyes
Regard me in fixed inquiring-wise
      As those of a soul that weighed,

Scarce consciously,
The eternal question of what Life was,
And why we were there, and by whose strange laws
      That which mattered most could not be.

---

* Florence Emily Dugdale.

138

"I SOMETIMES THINK"
(for f. e. h.)*

I sometimes think as here I sit
    Of things I have done,
Which seemed on doing not unfit
    To face the sun:
Yet never a soul has paused a whit
    On such—not one.

There was that eager strenuous press
    To sow good seed;
There was that saving from distress
    In the nick of need;
There were those words in the wilderness:
    Who cared to heed?

Yet can this be full true, or no?
    For one did care,
And, spiriting into my house, to, fro,
    Like wind on the stair,
Cares still, heeds all, and will, even though
    I may despair.

---

* Florence Hardy.

A POET

Attentive eyes, fantastic heed,
Assessing minds, he does not need,
Nor urgent writs to sup or dine,
Nor pledges in the rosy wine.

For loud acclaim he does not care
By the august or rich or fair,
Nor for smart pilgrims from afar,
Curious on where his hauntings are.

But soon or later, when you hear
That he has doffed this wrinkled gear,
Some evening, at the first star-ray,
Come to his graveside, pause and say:

"Whatever his message—glad or grim—
Two bright-souled women clave to him";
Stand and say that while day decays;
It will be word enough of praise.

July 1914.

THE WEST-OF-WESSEX GIRL

A very West-of-Wessex girl,
    As blithe as blithe could be,
    Was once well-known to me,
And she would laud her native town,
    And hope and hope that we
Might sometime study up and down
    Its charms in company.

But never I squired my Wessex girl
    In jaunts to Hoe or street
    When hearts were high in beat,
Nor saw her in the marbled ways
    Where market-people meet
That in her bounding early days
    Were friendly with her feet.

Yet now my West-of-Wessex girl,
    When midnight hammers slow
    From Andrew's, blow by blow,
As phantom draws me by the hand
    To the place—Plymouth Hoe—
Where side by side in life, as planned,
    We never were to go!

Begun in Plymouth, March 1913.

"SHE OPENED THE DOOR"

She opened the door of the West to me,
    With it loud sea-lashings,
    And cliff-side clashings
Of waters rife with revelry.

She opened the door of Romance to me,
    The door from a cell
    I had known too well,
Too long, till then, and was fain to flee.

She opened the door of a Love to me,
    That passed the wry
    World-welters by
As far as the arching blue the lea.

She opens the door of the Past to me,
    Its magic lights,
    Its heavenly heights,
When forward little is to see!

1913.

INDEX TO FIRST LINES

INDEX TO TITLES